Ms. P's GUIDE TO GOING TO HELL

BABS PARKER

Copyright © 2020 by Barbara Purbaugh

All rights reserved. No part of this book may be reproduced or used in any manner without written permission of the copyright owner except for the use of quotations in a book review.

FIRST EDITION

Interior Design: Natalia Junqueira (Dawn Book Design)

Acknowledgements

A huge thank you to the following people:

My therapist, Liz, (This book would not be possible without her encouragement.)

My family members especially my mother, my aunt, H., and my aunt, S.

My friends

My former students

My "ex-husbands"

My neighbor, Anne

Men on internet dating sites

Random strangers

And all the other characters who made these ten years an interesting adventure.

Table of Contents

Prologue	*6*
NASCARed again	*7*
Sex and other awkward things	*19*
How do I get a man like that?	*29*
Internet dating	*37*
Young Indian Men	*46*
Exploding Vaginas	*49*
Going to Hell	*55*
My eggs are old.	*63*
The sisters	*69*
Feminist Rants	*88*
They're hungry, and it makes them mean.	*92*
Gamma Rays	*110*
Working on my porn website	*115*
My "ex-husbands"	*120*
White Vans	*129*
It's just umbrellas.	*141*
The Official Drink of the Psych Ward	*151*
Loud, Opinionated Women	*159*
Adventures in Teaching	*172*
Friends don't let friends mullet.	*188*

Old Lady Things	*194*
My therapist says...	*204*
Encounters	*213*
My friends and family will understand.	*219*
Epilogue	*224*

Prologue

For years, people have been coming up to me and saying, "I love your Facebook posts. They're so funny."

And then my Facebook friend, William Prystauk, suggested that I create a book of my posts.

I laughed at the idea. Who would read that?

But sadly, it planted a seed, a very dark seed.

This is the book, a hodge-podge of ten years of my life, ages 41-51. I admit it is self-indulgent. I shamelessly want people to laugh at my jokes.

And after I'm dead, when people ask, "What was Babs like?"

A feminist spinster? A cat lady with no cats? A foul-mouthed smut peddler?

I just want you to hand them this book; it explains it all.

Chapter 1

NASCARed again

I sometimes forget where I'm from. I'm having a conversation with someone, and suddenly, I hit a big brick wall of redneck ignorance.

There should be a word for that.

I was talking to Jethro, and I got rednecked again.

I was talking to Jethro, and I got white-trashed again.

I was talking to Jethro, and I got camouflaged again.

I was talking to Jethro, and I got NASCARed again.

Oh, yeah, that's it. It's going around and around in circles and hitting a wall. Yep, I got NASCARed again.

No matter what you may have heard, the first day of deer season is NOT a religious holiday.

Thank goodness for the hide button on Facebook. I won't have to look at the photos of dead deer during hunting season.

Why does the internet send me ads for camouflage wedding dresses? That's like two of my worst nightmares together.

I went to Walmart. There were a lot of people there, but I didn't see them because they were all wearing camouflage.

I want to live in a place where no one wears camouflage.

Why do you wear camouflage to go fishing?

Someone once told me that people in Greensburg, Pennsylvania, were so much more sophisticated than people in Somerset, Pennsylvania. I worked in Greensburg all week.

This was a conversation I overheard.

"Educated" accountant: You know that movie where they're slaves, and there is a young girl.

Co-worker: You mean *The Help*. They weren't slaves. There was segregation, but they got paid.

"Educated" accountant: Well, slaves got paid. Didn't they?

Oh, and everyone in the office, everyone, said gum band instead of rubber band.

I heard "Educated" accountant on the phone to a client: We'll just gum band them together.

It makes me kind of proud to be so unsophisticated.

Johnstown, Pennsylvania, is like a one-night stand: beautiful at night, not so hot in the daylight.

I was in Michaels, and this lady approached me and started asking me about her craft project, the snowman Olaf made from marshmallows. We read the decorations on the baking stuff.

Her: I was going to make his eyebrows with magic marker.

Me: Are the kids eating these?

Her: Yes.

Me: Then you don't want to use magic marker.

Her: It's just a little bit.

We found edible markers.

But that explains a lot about the kids in Johnstown; doesn't it?

People, we live in the mountains of Pennsylvania. It's going to snow, and the forecast was for like three inches. Geez, stop acting like men. Three inches ain't that impressive, and there's no need to get excited.

Woohoo! Ten inches. Oh, wait, you mean snow. Damn it!

Chapter 2

Sex and other awkward things

Other people look at clouds and see Jesus.

I see penises.

Earthquake in Pennsylvania

A little vibration without batteries is God's way of saying he loves us and wants us to be happy.

Earthquake in D.C.

I hate when your giant phallic symbol cracks.

I was having lunch with my family, and my purse, kind of open, was sitting next to me in the booth. These two little kids came to sit in the booth next to us.

My sister: Do you have anything in your purse that would scare small children?

Me: No.

My brother-in-law: Anything rubber?

Me: I don't carry that around.

Geez, what did they think I had?

I just used the word dildo in Words with Friends. My work on Earth is complete.

One of the worst parts about the laundromat is folding your underwear in public. In the movies, it's sexy, involving hot men and thongs. There is nothing sexy about granny panties.

Don't have sex with your neighbor. People in your neighborhood will think you're a whore.

Take that shit two blocks over, and no one will care.

I just got an iPhone. I'm so excited. It's like I have a penis; I can't stop playing with it.

I put together a desk all by myself with a newly purchased cordless screwdriver. It's the first power tool I've ever owned, and I now know why men love power tools. It must be what it feels like to have a penis; I just want to go around screwing things.

I visited the Jennie Wade House in Gettysburg. There's a legend that if you put your ring finger in the bullet hole that killed Jennie you will be married within a year, apparently because she didn't get to marry her sweetheart. I laughed out loud.

A year later, seeing as I did not get married, I said, "I'm writing a strongly worded letter."

My sister, Tammy, looked at me and said, "Come on, if all it took was sticking your finger in a hole, we'd have been married a long time ago."

Chapter 3

How do I get a man like that?

I was watching "Criminal Minds".

This guy has a one-night stand with a girl, and he promises to call.

Then he's killed by a serial killer. I'm going to assume that's what happened to all the men who never called me.

I was talking to one of my co-workers about dating younger men.

She looked at me.

Me: Don't worry; my cougar program is catch and release.

Me: My love life is like a community college; everyone gets in.

My friend: Maybe you need a placement test.

So, I'm 47 and single, and I love Valentine's Day.

I used to hate Valentine's Day. I remember one Valentine's Day working in an office, and every woman got flowers sent to her but me. Every desk had them but mine. I felt like a female Charlie Brown.

But I also remember the moment I began to like Valentine's Day again. It was one of those cold, gray days in Pennsylvania. I remember being in the store and seeing all the reds and pinks and thinking, what if Valentine's Day is just a need for color in a bleak, cold time?

I thought back to those wonderful times when I was a kid, and I made valentines for people. I wasn't hung up on them being perfect or right. I didn't care if I got one back. I just wanted someone to feel loved.

That's the problem with being single too long with too many failed relationships. You begin to see love as something that was not given but something that was taken and never returned.

I took back Valentine's Day. Instead of waiting for that right person, I gave cards to people I loved, and I began to see Valentine's Day as a day to give my love to people who deserved it, who would appreciate it, and who would return it.

It was not a day for being ashamed of your failed love. It was a day to celebrate love, and I have a lot of people I love and who love me. And that love deserves appreciation every day, but in the bleak coldness of February, we, sometimes, need an extra reminder of the warmth of love.

And I'll be honest; I'm a romantic. Sometimes, we're afraid to admit we're romantic because we'll be perceived as weak or naive or even foolish. But I have been a fool for love before, and I can tell you that, even though those relationships didn't work out, each of them had a moment that reminded me of how amazing love can be.

And the most amazing kind of love is love for yourself, and so many people carelessly toss that aside in exchange for the love of another. I know a lot of smart, loving, motivated women who are in relationships with men who are not their intellectual equals, who are lazy (and I don't mean a job), or are just plain mean.

Stop bemoaning the lack of a man and start appreciating yourself. Give yourself a hug; pamper yourself because today you knew your worth. You knew those flowers or that last-minute box of chocolate could never equal the feeling of knowing who you are and loving her.

Take today to pamper yourself and take a moment of that day to tell someone, anyone, you love them.

I just want you to know that you are loved. Enjoy your Valentine's Day.

> P.S. Although this was written for women, it can apply to men, too.

For those of you feeling sad on Valentine's Day, remember these things:

1. Ice cream prefers chubby chicks.
2. A pint of ice cream doesn't try to tell you it is a gallon.
3. Ice cream is always good in bed.

Facebook keeps suggesting dating websites. I feel very uncomfortable that they're trying to find me a boyfriend.

I know some guys who just let horrible, bitchy women walk all over them. Why? And most importantly, how do I get a man like that?

Chapter 4

Internet dating

My friends and their great success stories convinced me to try internet dating again.

Here's what I got. I'm not making this up. Feel free to laugh 'cause this is some funny shit.

One actual date

Young guys who said things like this. "People don't date anymore. They hang out."

A guy who sent me a message that didn't make sense. When I said I didn't understand the message, he said, "I'm out of my medicine for anxiety and depression. You seem like a nice person."

I said, "I am nice. You get your meds straightened out, and then we'll talk."

He said, "Yes, ma'am."

I talked to a guy for two weeks, and then he said, "There are no eligible women in my area."

One guy who said, "When can I suck your toes?"

This message: "Hi, this is Kim. My fiancé is Paul. Are you into couples?"

Several unsolicited pictures of penises. I'm 45 and single. I've seen a few. Yours isn't that impressive.

And by the way, why would you think that was charming or acceptable?

And finally, a guy who thought it was perfectly acceptable to call me sugar tits. I have never in my 45 years been called sugar tits, and I've dated some losers. Who thinks that's okay? Who, besides Mel Gibson, says that? And that, ladies and gentlemen, is why I'm still single.

Today's Internet Dating Message

"Wanna hump it and dump it?"

Today's Internet Dating Message

"Can I lick your butt hole?"

I think this is one of those rare occasions when I'm at a loss for words. I don't even know what to say to that.

Today's Internet Dating Message

Him: I'm working on my relationship with Jesus.

Me: That's good. Spirituality is important.

Pause

Sends me a penis picture

Me: I don't think that's what Jesus would do.

Internet Dating Pick-up Line

"Santa made you a toy for Christmas but dropped it at the wrong place. Would you like to get your boy toy?"

Today's Internet Dating Conversation

Guy: What's the secret to your beauty?

Me: I bathe in the blood of virgins I meet while internet dating...

Today's Internet Dating Conversation

Dude on the internet: Are you always this hot or did you just steal the sun?

Me: I'm always this hot, but that could be the menopause.

There's an organization called Best Buddies. My student said her duties there were to "Be a friend to a person with mental disabilities."

I call this dating.

Chapter 5

Young Indian Men

Young Indian men really like me. I bet I could be a supermodel in India, or, at least, a porn star.

Today, I saw so many pretty young Indian (from India) men.

That being said, when you see a really pretty man, on a scale of one to ten, one being he'll like it and ten being I'll go to jail, how inappropriate is it to just walk up and lick him?

I got a voicemail message this morning. "Did you just post on Facebook that you want to lick young Indian men?"

Chapter 6

Exploding Vaginas

Facebook suggested I join this group: Lesbian Audiobooks. I'm not sure what that means.

Have they given up on finding me a boyfriend?

I deeply, deeply mistrust anyone who can't be located when you google their name.

I got a Twitter account.

Me: I have followers. I always wanted a cult.

My niece: Nine followers does not make a cult.

Me: It takes time. Jim Jones didn't start with Jonestown.

When I was young, in the days of rotary phones and party lines, I remember having a conversation about the fact that someday we would have video phones, and that seemed so far off and futuristic. This morning, I taught an English lesson to a student in Russian via Skype, and I realized the future is now. Makes you wonder what will happen next. I'm hoping it's my holodeck.

I was in a meeting at work, and my cell phone rang. My ringtone is Spock saying, "Live long and prosper." I could not find my phone. I stood up to look for it. It was in my bra.

I reached inside my bra, pulled out the phone, shut it off, and said, "Now you know where Babs keeps her valuables."

Of course, they laughed. No professionalism but a funny story.

Listen, people, stop with the chain letter posts. You know those posts: If I share this, I'll get money. If I don't, my hair will fall out; I'll get boils; my vagina will explode or whatever. They make me uncomfortable. I'm already going to hell for my wicked ways. I don't need the added pressure of an exploding vagina if I don't forward a horoscope.

Chapter 7

Going to Hell

Those Facebooks posts with Jesus knocking on the door that say, "Share if you'd let him in."

Who the fuck wouldn't answer the door for Jesus?

Seriously, if Jesus comes to the door, you'll want to know what he has to say.

Oh God, the Mormons are in the library, sitting at the computers next to me. I hope they don't try to tell me about Jesus.

My freshman students didn't know what Judgment Day was. I had to explain Armageddon and the Four Horsemen of the Apocalypse and The Rapture with the dead rising, all so they could understand some poetry. How do they not know this? Am I really the person who should teach the Bible? Well, it was the going to hell part. I'm qualified for that part.

Two of the whitest people I have ever seen came to my door today with two of the whitest kids I have ever seen, and they had Bibles in their hands. Oh shit, I thought, they're going to try and save me.

They were looking for my neighbor.

Wait, what?

You're not going to offer to pray for me, tell me the good news, try and save me? Geez, even they've given up on me. Fuck, now I know I'm going to hell.

This is a serious question. Apologies to Catholics. But is there a patron saint you pray to if you want to get laid? I know. I know. They want you find a spouse and have babies, but you know, secretly, is there like a get lucky saint?

Yes, I do have too much time and the internet. And yes, I do hear all my Catholic friends praying to the saint of lost causes right now. And yes, I'm going to hell.

If St. Jude's Hospital sends you address labels and you don't donate, but you use them, you're going to hell; aren't you?

Me (at Sheetz): I'm sorry that you have to work on Easter, but I promise you that God wants me to have this doughnut.

Sheetz employee of the year: Well, if it's God's will

Later, I forget to remove my debit card.

Me: I'm sorry

Sheetz employee of the year: You are forgiven.

Me: Thank you, Father, for I have sinned.

It's comforting to know when I get to hell, they'll be a Sheetz there.

In today's edition of why I'm going to hell

When I ask how your baby is, I'm being polite. I don't really care. I mean I care like I don't want your kid to get hit by a bus or get baby cancer or anything, but I don't really need to know the details of their life.

Some people have cute babies like so sweet I want to eat them up (not in the Hansel and Gretel way), but some people have really ugly babies. I like those babies more. Those babies are like Goth babies, horrifyingly cool.

Stop dressing your ugly kid in pink and blue; get that kid some black. Embrace the ugly! This concludes Going to Hell: The Baby Edition.

Chapter 8

My eggs are old.

Today, someone asked me why I don't want children. Why are people still asking me about having kids? What age do I have to reach before they understand basic biology?

Do I have to explain that my fucking eggs are old, and there's only a 1% chance that a woman over the age of 45 can get pregnant. Thank you, God! That ship has sailed.

The x-ray tech asked if I was pregnant.
Me: No, I'm 47. That ship has sailed.
Him: We have to ask until you're 50.
Me: Woohoo, only 3 more years.

The most horrifying job title ever...birthday party attendant.

That just reeks of sticky hands and snot.

The dumbest thing said to me today, "My thirty-year-old daughter needs to have a baby, so she'll learn that the world doesn't revolve around her."

One of my Facebook friends was complaining about only getting macaroni art for Mother's Day, and she wanted a spa day.

Here was my response.

Okay, you know I love my mother, and I love and appreciate all moms. I know you have a hard job to do. But let's be honest. You didn't do anything special. Most kids are here because someone fucked up the birth control, and come on, you live in a society that gives you rewards for being a baby making machine.

You want to do something hard? Try being childless. Try 20+ years, of being asked, "When are you having kids?" Try getting the sympathy look when you say you don't have kids. Try sitting though endless baby showers being talked down to like you're somehow special needs because you don't have children, and then when you get "too old" to have children, try hearing about how you live with your cats. Fuck you, assholes. I don't have any cats.

And let's be honest. Although I was probably just as lucky about birth control as you were unlucky, frankly, I made a choice. I didn't want to bring a baby into the world if I couldn't financially support it or I had a fucked-up partner or a fucked-up life. By not being a mother, I was a more responsible mother than some of the mothers that I know. And I loved your kids. I sat through the same games, school plays, and sticky kid birthday parties that you did. I changed diapers. I was the person you called when you wanted to kill your kid, and I talked you out of killing your kid. Am I getting a Mother's Day card for that shit? No, I'm not.

Do I regret not having children? No. I made a choice and so did you. So, guess what you don't get for being a mother? You don't get to sleep in or a free parking space. You don't get to do what you want. You can't stop being a mom. It's a lifetime commitment. What do you get? You get another human being who comes into the world loving you unconditionally. Do you know how amazing that is? Unconditionally so don't fuck it up. That's it; just don't fuck it up. Take your macaroni necklace and your two-for-one Applebee's coupons (or whatever you people do on Mother's Day) and be grateful. There are a lot of women who would give anything to be a mother.

Chapter 9

The sisters

My mom does this all day long.

Her: What is this?

Me: A banana

Her: Why is it here? What are you going to do with it?

Me: It's in my lunch bag. I'm going to eat it.

Her: What is this?

Me: A pen

Her: Why is it here? What are you going to do with it?

Me: Write you a note.

I swear one of these days...

Her: What is this?

Me: A dildo

Her: Why is it here? What are you going to do with it?

Me: Well, Mom...

I woke up, and I was greeted by my mom.

Her: I dropped my gum in the toaster. I need help cleaning it out.

I clean the gum out of the toaster. I'm not sure how that happened, and I don't want to know.

My mom: I'm going to sleep. You can do what you want.

Me: I'm going to run amok.

My mom: Don't eat the candy; it's for the kids trick-or-treating.

Me: (eating the candy) I'll go knock on the door if it makes you feel better.

My mom: I brushed my teeth.
Me: The doctor is looking at your who-ha.
Her: I don't want to have bad breath.

Her: Is this outfit okay?
Me: The doctor is looking at your who-ha.
Her: I washed it twice.
Me: I did not need to know that.

I went for a walk with my aunt, S.

Her: Barbie, walk closer to me.

I think she's worried about falling.

Her: I farted and want to blame it on you.

Yesterday, I handed my aunt, S., the newspaper.

Her: Am I in it?

Me: I didn't read the police report.

Her: I didn't get caught.

Aunt S.: When I drank, I only had a couple of slow Jims.

Me: I've had a few slow Jims myself.

Last night, my aunt, S., wondered how many calories are in her breakfast.

Me: You're 79. Does it matter?

She laughed.

Me: I'm eating an apple.

Aunt S.: I got that fruit for being old.

Me: What?

Her: The church gives it to old people. This is the first year I got it. I'm finally old enough.

My aunt, S.: If you're hungry, I see there's a tiny can of wieners in the cupboard.

Me: No one wants tiny wieners.

Her: Yeah, no one wants tiny wieners in their mouth.

How my aunt, S., greets me

"I ate a hot pepper. It burned my mouth, and when I went to the bathroom, hot, hot, hot."

When I stay with my aunt, S., she likes to give me money. I always put it back when she goes to sleep.

Tonight, it was $20.

Then, it was $20 more.

Then, it was one lucky penny.

Then it was $1.47 in change.

This time, I'm keeping the lucky penny.

Also, she gives me ice cream. I always eat the ice cream.

Me: I have a key to your house. Don't worry about it.

My aunt, S.: You better knock before you come in. I might be in here doing it with my boyfriend.

Me: That's why I always yell your name when I walk in.

Her: You don't want to see that.

Me: No but I'd say good for you.

We laughed. She has no boyfriend.

When I leave my aunt, S.'s, house, I say, "Behave."
She looks at me like 'are you kidding?'.
I say, "Okay, I won't either."
We laugh.

Backstory: My aunt, H., is 76. She was married to her husband since she was 18, and he died within the last year. This guy in town keeps saying he's my aunt's boyfriend, which makes us laugh.

Yesterday, I was going to the other house my aunt owns.

Her: Don't mind the guy with the urinals.

I went into the house. This guy was coming out with actual porcelain urinals.

Him: Don't mind me. I'm the guy with the urinals.

Me: If it's your thing, I'm not judging.

A couple of hours later, I went back to her house.

Her: What have you been doing over there with my boyfriend?

We laughed.

Me: (shocked) Wait, the urinal guy is your boyfriend? He's handsome and like maybe 60. Oh, you got a boy toy.

And we laughed.

My aunt, H., misses her husband.

Her: No one to talk to.
No one to argue with.
No one to boss around.

Me: It's really the third one. Right?

My aunt, H, called me tonight and said she was at the pharmacy in Meyersdale, and someone asked her if she was the crazy aunt in my posts.

Me: (laughing): You're one of them.

Her: I didn't know what she was talking about but said yes, I am.

I explained that I didn't say anything personal, just funny conversations.

Now, I'm not sure if she thinks she's a celebrity or she's afraid I'm telling all of her personal business on the internet.

Aunt S.: You can still get married.

Aunt H.: And when you do, you'll feel like a lark. (Happy songbird)

Me: Well, I'd be happy because I will be witnessing a miracle.

Chapter 10

Feminist Rants

I get wedding pictures and baby pictures, but when did engagement and maternity portraits become a thing?

I'm going to do single portraits. Then I'm going to throw a big "I didn't get married" reception, and you have to buy me lots of presents. But first, I want a "I'm still a bachelorette" party (although words with -ette at the end seem demeaning), which also involves gifts.

Then I'm going to wait a year to have more pictures taken and announce my non-pregnancy, which might actually be a "Congratulations, you're too fucking old to have babies" party. Again, this will require lots of presents.

I know what you're going to say, I'm bitter, or Babs, these are milestones in a person's life; they should be celebrated. Well, I think graduating college is a milestone. I did it three times. I didn't see my big college reception, and I damn sure didn't see any of you throwing me a graduation shower!

Is there a point? Yes, what kind of a message are we sending to young girls when we only celebrate milestones related to marriage and maternity?

I told my Tech Writing students about making eye contact during a speech.

I said, "Choose three people, but make sure it's safe people, not your buddy who will make you laugh. The girls are usually a good choice because girls are conditioned to be nice."

One of my students raised his hand and said, "Who conditioned you?"

I hate when you go to a restaurant alone, and they ask if you want to sit at the bar.

No, bitch, I want to sit in a booth like all the smug marrieds with their crotch goblins and/or the people with friends.

I need space for my vast loneliness.

I'm not Mrs. Parker. I am not married. My identity should not be defined by my marital status. I should not be defined by my connection, or lack thereof, to a man.

This concludes today's feminist rant.

Chapter 11

They're hungry, and it makes them mean.

Just ate a Klondike bar, and I didn't have to do anything for it. Thank you, feminist movement.

I like working with women. We have snacks. Correct me if I'm wrong, but I don't think men bring snacks.

My friend: Are you okay, anxiety-laden Barbie?

Me: This is what it's like to be my friend. You laugh at my jokes, listen to me whine about my problems, participate and/or appreciate my shenanigans, and eat snacks.

Him: I love snacks!

I am 50 years old. The most important life skill I've learned: always have snacks.

Today, I thought about murdering a lot of people, but now, I'm getting free crazy bread from Little Caesar's, so that plan is on hold.

Food on the floor – Five-second rule

Food found in your bra - No time limit especially if it's chocolate

There comes that magical moment in every woman's life.

When you have your period and you are about to murder someone, and then you find a candy bar at the bottom of your purse.

Oreos are like crack. Just one, then it's two, and then pretty soon you're trading sexual favors for the double stuff.

Conversation with my stomach almost every night

Stomach: Bitch, I'm hungry. Make dinner.

Me: There's nothing to microwave.

Stomach: Bitch, you can cook.

 Me: But that's hard work. Can't we just eat a cookie?

Stomach: Bitch, I ain't...wait, did you say cookie?

Girl Scouts selling cookies in Kroger

Me: All right, you little cookie pushers, I'll take 2 of these.

Everyone laughed, but that might have gone horribly wrong. You know, scaring small children and such.

Today's conversation

My boss: Babs, do you cook meals for yourself in the evening?

Me: Yes, simple ones.

Her: Since my father died, my elderly mother doesn't want to cook or only wants to eat out. I think she's depressed.

She paused.

Her: But that has nothing to do with you cooking.

Wait, what? Did she just compare me to her depressed elderly mother?

8:00 AM and the smoke detector is going off.
Don't panic. Babs is just cooking again.

There's a doughnut wagon in front of a car wash. There's no way that can be a bad thing. Right?

Who has a morning meeting and doesn't have doughnuts? I can't work under these conditions.

I went for a walk and found ten dollars. Guess exercise does pay.

As I was walking a mile today, I decided I wanted to organize a 1K walk. It will only be for overweight people. It will not be timed. The goal will be to finish. At the end, you get a slice of cake, and we'll call it the cake walk. All proceeds will go to some organization that promotes acceptance. The whole idea will be that it's okay if you're not skinny. You can still be active even if you're overweight. Too often overweight people are discouraged about exercise because it's often presented to us by screaming super-hungry skinny people who judge us. Exercise without judgment. That's nice.

For all those women who put lose weight on their New Year's Resolution list:

I spent a great deal of my adult life worrying about being fat.

What I should have known was that fat people can exercise. That exercise does really make you feel better. That exercise isn't gym class. It's a walk down the street, gentle yoga, or dancing to a song.

What I should have known is boys or girls will like you, fat or not.

What I should have known was that my body belonged to me.

What I should have known was how to love myself, no matter what size I was.

I hurt my back and had to go to urgent care.

"Go to the gym. You'll have energy. You'll feel better," my skinny friends said.

They lie, and you know why they lie. They're hungry, and it makes them mean.

Chapter 12

Gamma Rays

I needed an MRI of my back. The problem with the MRI wasn't being stuck in a tube; it was the loud noise. At times, it sounded like the red alert on a "Star Trek" ship. I was a bit concerned that there might be an alien attack.

Also, I asked for classic country music on the headphones. The first song was "Ring of Fire" by Johnny Cash. "I fell into a burning ring of fire" is not what you want to hear as they're sliding you into a tube.

I felt kind of sick after my MRI.

Me: I think it was all the gamma rays they shot through me.

My brother: You're not the Incredible Hulk. They didn't use gamma rays.

Me: You don't know.

Your doctor, even if he is a medical student, should not wear skinny jeans.

At the doctor's office, I just found out that my purse weighs seven pounds. Something seems wrong about that.

I pulled a muscle.

The x-ray technician: Where is the pain?

Me: Between my boobs, for want of a more medical term.

Him: I'll write breast on the report.

Me: I think writing boobs will get you fired.

We laughed.

He takes the x-rays.

Him: You say the pain is also under your breast.

Me: I'm greatly disappointed that you didn't say boob.

And we laughed. But I may have sexually harassed the x-ray technician.

Chapter 13

Working on my porn website

I tell my doctor I am still looking for a job.

Her: Isn't there a prayer you can say to get a job?

Me: I'm sure there is.

Her: My mother needed to sell her house, so she said a prayer and buried a saint by her front door.

Me: I'll bury whoever you want if it gets me a job.

Me: If get the job in Arizona, I won't even need a car in the desert. I'll just get a moped.

My niece: Aunt Barb, your purse would make a moped tip over.

I have to answer this question for a job application: "Give me an example of when you thought outside of the box."

I have never thought in the box. I don't know where the damn box is.

The hardest writing assignment ever for a job application: In 125 characters, why are you unique?

I had 125 words before I read it was characters. Damn it.

My friend suggested, "Trust me; you never met a motherfucker like me before."

I'm tempted.

I swear if one more person asks me what I'm doing with my time since I'm unemployed, I'm going to tell them working on my porn website.

Chapter 14

My "ex-husbands"

My roommates watch cooking shows like they're porn. They convinced me to watch a cooking show because the chef was making doughnuts. The chef makes muffins with sugar and cinnamon sprinkled on them.

Me: I think I speak for all fat people. If you tell me you're making doughnuts and feed me muffins, we're fighting.

I go downstairs for a snack.

Mick and Guy, my roommates, are arguing about building a house.

Mick: Say Barbara's your contractor...

Me: I just came for a snack. I'm not building anything.

Later, Guy leaves the room.

Mick: He's quitting us.

Me: (quoting *Brokeback Mountain*) He can't quit us.

I then explain the quote and how the movie is a beautiful love story.

Me: I'm leaving. I came for a snack, not Brokeback Contracting.

This results in a hilarious conversation about our potential reality show, which because they are both divorced, we'll call, The ex-husbands of Powhatan.

Me: You'll have to do the love scenes or maybe have a lot of sexual tension.

Guy: We already have that.

They're both straight men in their early 60s, so they were slightly uncomfortable like boys in middle school.

I gave them crap like you're definitely a bottom. I mentioned lube, and they both tightened their butt checks.

Now, I call them "my ex-husbands".

One of my "ex-husbands", Mick, gets a Sports Illustrated, the swimsuit issue.

Me: They still do that?

Him: Yes.

Me: You know they have this thing called the internet that has porn.

Him: They don't have Christie Brinkley.

Guy's actual ex-wife: You know she's sixty years old.

They argue about it for a few minutes.

Actual ex-wife: Yeah, that's not her face. She's had work done.

Me: And nobody's body looks like that at 60.

He gets annoyed and starts to leave the room.

Me: Sorry, we ruined your fantasy.

My "ex-husbands" were talking about a beer called Old Chub

Mick: It's as nasty as its name.

Me: It sounds like a guy you wake up next to after a one-night stand.

They laugh.

Me: You know it's true. You've done it.

The guys deny it but look at each other like they both know it's true, but they won't admit it in front of the Guy's actual ex-wife, who is in the room.

Me: Well, I'm sorry that your life is so boring.

My "ex-husband", Guy, said he had a girlfriend, and he couldn't decide whether or not to break up with her because she made great pickled beets. This is not the first time he's said he had trouble breaking up with a woman for a bizarre reason.

Me: Do you have a list of these women somewhere?

Him: Like an Excel spreadsheet?

Me: Yeah, I'd loved to read it. I could write a list too, but almost every name would be followed with jerk.

Him: I'm sure I'm on someone's list like that.

I was talking to my "ex-husband", Mick, about sloppy joes. He gives me crap about Manwich.

He started talking about eating sloppy joes with a bun when he was a kid.

Me: You had buns. You must have been rich.

He laughed.

Him: How do you even eat sloppy joes on bread?

Me: It ain't pretty.

Rich kids

My "ex-husbands" made me a good-bye dinner.

Mick: This dinner is going to be so good my nipples are hard.

Guy: As long as you keep it at the tits and don't go any lower.

Texting with my "ex-husband", Mick

Me: I hear Hurricane Florence is giving you guys a real blow job? Lmao

Him: She is about to ... or so they say. You never know you are going to get one until it actually happens.

Me: Like blow jobs.

Today's message

Him: We aren't even getting a reach around from Flo.

Guy gave me food, then he said, "I've got to make a phone call, so I'm going to have to leave you alone."

Me: I'm not responsible for what happens when I'm unsupervised.

Him: Don't play with matches.

Chapter 15

White Vans

For my werewolf book, I just had to google how long it takes to burn a body. I hope no one checks my search history.

"Slowly poisoning someone" is in my search history. Yes, I'm a writer, and yes, I do have a therapist.

My friend, who also grew up in Garrett: You should write a murder mystery.

Me: Set in Garrett?

Him: Yes, someone dies, and everyone else is jealous.

I was sleeping quite peacefully, wonderfully even, until my neighbor decided that 1:00 AM would be a great time to move what I can only assume were the bodies from his car to his garage.

Why in scary movies do people go to the boiler room? I don't think in my life I've ever encountered a boiler room, and if I did, I wouldn't go in there.

This is the message I get from my caring brother:

Him: I'm just checking to see if you're alive, or do I have to get a dumpster to throw away your valuable stuff? If I don't hear from you in three to five days, I know I'll have to get a dumpster.

Me: Three to five days? My corpse would be pretty ripe by then.

I called him to tell him no dumpster is needed yet.

What color did you dye your hair?

Me: Lifetime movie: main character running from the law dyes her hair in the bathroom of a seedy motel on the wrong side of town

Apparently, 3:30 AM is the perfect time for your smoke alarm to announce, "Low battery!" in a very loud, very creepy female robot voice.

Well, at least, I know I won't die in a fire, maybe a heart attack but never a fire.

I hate winter.

I just had the thought that I could stay in my house forever if I had supplies.

I am seriously in danger of becoming the Unabomber.

Six hundred dollars and I can buy a white van, perfect for kidnapping, serial killing, and/or just living down by the river.

Someone asked me what I like to do for fun.

Me: Murder Hitchhikers.

Him: What's that?

Me: Murdering hitchhikers. It was big in the 70s.

Him: Cool.

He totally did not get that it was a joke, so I explained that I was joking, but please bail me out if he reports me.

This week in internet dating

Him: (as a way of introducing himself) I got no attachments and a van.

Me: Is the van white?

Him: Yes.

Me: Oh, so, you're a serial killer.

Him: It's cool. I got a bed in the back.

Me: So, you're homeless?

Him: I call it my whore van.

Me: I've seen that episode of "Criminal Minds".

Him: It's cool. Here's a picture.

Chapter 16

It's just umbrellas.

There are no knights in shining armor. No one is going to rescue you. And the truth is you don't need rescuing, you got this.

I had a great conversation with my niece, and I said, "Saying and doing things is like throwing a pebble into the water; it creates ripples. Sometimes, if you do or say the wrong thing, it creates negative ripples. Sometimes, if you do and say the right thing, it creates positive ripples. And the only thing we can do in life is do our best to create more positive ripples than negatives ones."

There is no cosmic scoreboard.

Bad people are going to continue to get away with being horrible excuses for human beings. If you're good, you're not going to be rewarded for being good. There will be no magical day in which all your suffering was for something greater.

You need to decide what kind of person you are going to be. Where is your moral compass?

My neighbor's business is mine because I am my brother's keeper. My neighbor's business is not mine because I am not their judge. There is a difference.

People are meant to be big, and every day, other people try and make them feel small.

If you wear your heart on your sleeve, someone's bound to wipe their nose on it.

Don't keep going back to the same well expecting water. If that well is dry, start digging a new well.

You can't complain about the fox destroying the henhouse if you invited the fox in.

At my job, when it rains, everyone loses their shit. We have lengthy conversations and extreme issues around umbrellas for guests. One day, I was getting involved in the umbrella drama, and I stopped myself and thought, It's just umbrellas, man. It's not heart surgery, and no one's going to die on the table. It's just umbrellas.

So, now, when I'm sweating the small stuff, I say, "It's just umbrellas. It's just umbrellas."

Sometimes, in life and love, you just need someone who will be kind to you. That's it, just kindness, and sometimes, the greatest kindness in a time of need comes from someone you hardly know or a stranger.

Chapter 17

The Official Drink of the Psych Ward

Extra light Kool-Aid Love

I went to a yoga therapy group for survivors of sexual abuse. At the first meeting, they asked me how I was.

I said, "I have pants on, and I'm out of bed, and that's all I got."

It was all I had.

When I thought of yoga, I thought of super-skinny, super-hungry women in leotards, forcing me into unnatural pretzel shapes.

I'm not wearing yoga pants, I thought.

"This isn't one of those groups like in *Fried Green Tomatoes* where you look at you who-ha," my friend asked.

I said no.

Although, honestly, at that time, I wasn't sure if that was going to happen or not.

I told my brother we were drumming.

He asked, "Did you join a cult?"

I told him, "I'm not going to buy into this hippie enlightened crap. I won't drink the Kool-Aid."

But I was suicidal, so I had nothing to lose. I found myself standing like a tree and putting rocks into water symbolizing letting go. I found myself screaming and chanting.

I found myself...

We had to write down on a piece of paper one good thing about everyone in the group.

The words I got back were smart, funny, full of fire, big, loving heart, leader. I had been viewing myself in a distorted funhouse mirror for so long that I thought that broken misshapen image was really me. I was now looking in the mirror they held. It was a better view. Here was a roomful of women who didn't just tolerate my weirdness but celebrated it and loved me for it. I had been accepted into the tribe.

And then one day, Rachel said, "God is in all of us."

I could easily see it in these women who had not only survived but also survived with grace, and in spite of the fact that life had shown them darkness and hate, they had light and love.

But I could not see it in me, Queen of Darkness, who loves Poe, reads Plath, and whose sarcastic tongue is sharp as a blade.

What did I know of light? What did I know about healing? What did I know of God?

Hadn't God abandoned me? Didn't God want to punish me? Hadn't God hated me as much as I hated myself?

For the first time in my life, the answer was no. For the first time in my life, I felt comfortable in my body. I felt comfortable in my mind. For the first time, I felt comfortable in my spirit.

So, I drank the Kool-Aid, every drop. And I'd drink it again and again. Kool-Aid extra light with love

P.S. We did not look at our who-has.

I was talking to my sister about the fact that I might have Oppositional Defiant Disorder.

She starts laughing: Oh yes.

Me: I'm serious.

Her: So am I.

I like to dress up when I go to see my psychiatrist.

That way, when she asks me, "Are you homicidal or suicidal? Do you think you have superpowers? Do you hear voices? Do you think life is worth living?"

I won't look like I'm depressed, hanging out in my sweats all day.

I don't have to see my shrink for four months, instead of three. Look at me! I got a gold star in crazy class.

I spent 72 hours in the Psych Ward.

They always ask you if you have a plan.

I had a plan: two freezer bags filled with pain pills. It was my stockpile. I knew how many there were. I googled what they would do. I even had a note.

When the ambulance and police showed up, they gathered all the pills.

After the 72 hours, on the way out the door, the nurse hands me the freezer bags filled with pain pills.

I asked her to destroy them.

She said, "You might need these."

I have to go to therapy, but I don't want to put on pants. I could be wrong, but showing up at therapy without your pants could be misconstrued as crazy.

Watching a TV show and a guy gets out of the mental hospital. He asks for ginger ale because he missed it. I call bullshit. Ginger ale is the official drink of the psych ward.

Chapter 18

Loud, Opinionated Women

I hate when people say suicide is a selfish act. Most people who are suicidal think "they'll get over it" or "they'll realize what a burden I was". They really see themselves as a burden to their loved ones.

And honestly, people who are suicidal aren't thinking of other people, not because they are selfish but because they are in pain, and they just want the pain to end.

One of the best things someone said to me after I was hospitalized for depression and suicidal thoughts was, "I want you to live." Not the "I'm mad about you wanting to die", but the simple truth that he wanted me to live.

Every time I see a movie or TV show that has a scene from Afghanistan and Iraq, I feel physically sick. I grew up with Vietnam vets, and I knew the pain war caused, but it always seemed distant until year after year veterans sat in my classroom. Their pain was palpable.

One year, I read a student's paper where he talked about killing for the first time. I asked my students what they thought the next line was. I got all those kill 'em cliché responses. The next line was about his devastation after killing someone.

So, when you honor veterans, remember that even though they are home, some of them are still fighting.

It's 4th of July, and I'm wearing red, white, and blue fingernail polish.

Growing up in the big town of Garrett, Pennsylvania, I had this neighbor named Anne. She would tell me about sex, witches, gossip about the people in town, etc. She seemed so glamorous and worldly.

As an adult, I realized she probably didn't make it beyond Ohio, and some of her birth control advice was not scientifically sound.

But one time, she said, "This girl's going to make it. She's going to do great things."

Every teenager should hear that at least once in their life.

Why the red, white, and blue fingernails? Every year on the Fourth of July, we wanted to paint our fingernails red, white, and blue. But the five and dime store never sold white nail polish, so we had to settle for red and blue nails.

Here's to Anne, one of the best storytellers I ever knew, I may not have done great things, but I have all the colors now!

Let's talk about beautiful. Most of my life, I thought I was ugly, hideous like the elephant man or something. Of course, that was drilled into my head by an abuser. And then one day, I read an article about Joan Rivers, and she said, "No man ever called me beautiful and all I wanted was to be beautiful."

This made me sad. So, I wondered about the word beautiful. When we say it, we mean beautiful as in how society defines beauty, and very few people will ever meet that standard. So, I accepted that I was not beautiful.

But I acknowledged that I was attractive, which is different than beauty. Being attractive means people are drawn to you. It can be because spiritually you're a beautiful person. It can be because you have a great sense of humor. It can be because you have a self-confidence, and you own the room when you walk into it.

Think about the people you are drawn to. Why are you drawn to them? Bet, 99% of the time, it has nothing to do with them being physically "beautiful". Now, what makes you attractive? And if you don't know, I bet someone else can tell you. Let them.

Today is International Women's Day, and I wanted to celebrate all the women that have and continue to be in my life. My most meaningful relationships have been and continue to be with the long list of women who I have been blessed to know and love.

My biological sisters and my spiritual sisters

Women who have disabilities that face pain and struggle, but they wake up every day with a strength of spirit I would never possess.

Women who are survivors of abuse that have taken their pain and used it to help others Counselors who have saved my life a million times in a million ways, large and small. Women who care for aging parents

Women who are aging with dignity and hilarity

Bold young women who will be the voice of a new future

Women who are mothers and grandmothers

My mother and the women who have mothered and mentored me

Women who cannot or do not have children of their own but give that love to others every day

Women who raise disabled children with fierce love

Women who are teachers who sacrifice and struggle every day to make a difference in a student's life

Women who are nurses giving tender comfort to all the brave women I know facing illnesses especially cancer

Women who are no longer on this Earth but rest gently in my heart

Women who have experienced the loss of a loved one and shaped that loss into a legacy to honor that love

All the women who faced heartbreak and the end of relationships but never stop believing in love

Women who face fear and rejection from others yet love who they love proudly and powerfully

Women writers and artists who gave me a safe space to develop my own words and voice and gave me their words and art in return

The women who are loud

The women who lead

The women who made me laugh

And those that made me cry

Women who empowered me when I felt powerless.

Women who loved me when I was completely undeserving of their love.

Thank you to all these women! The world needs your light. Continue to shine!

What "Star Trek", Spock, and Leonard Nimoy taught us

"Star Trek" taught us that a world with all races working together was possible.

"Star Trek" taught us that women could be equal, valued members of the crew. "Star Trek" taught us that love and sexual attraction are color blind. "Star Trek" taught us that friendship was as essential for survival as was leadership. It taught us to be adventurous and curious, to want to know about other people and their cultures. It taught us that we could do amazing things with technology. Granted, there are some negative things because it was a TV show of its time. But it still taught us so many things.

Spock with his distant, analytical attempts to understand humans and human behavior made us look at who we are and why we behave the way we do. He taught us to not only feel but also that it was okay to feel. Spock taught us how to be human. That's why the show has been around for years because, sadly, these lessons need repeated.

That is why marking the passing of Leonard Nimoy is important. If you are of a certain age, you remember the show "In search of…". That was Leonard Nimoy teaching us, helping us to be curious about the world and its mysteries.

Leonard Nimoy could have walked away from the character of Spock. I know the cynical among you will say it was his bread and butter. But he could have walked away, but, instead, he not only embraced Spock, but he also made Spock better.

In the 2009 *Star Trek* movie, when Leonard Nimoy as Spock says, "I have been emotionally compromised." Every one of us felt that loss deeply. Just as we now feel the loss of Leonard deeply. Just as we feel the loss of Spock deeply. Once before, we lost Spock, but he came back to us. This time, we know he's not coming back, and we are left with a void. I think it would be a great tribute to Spock and to Leonard Nimoy if we truly learned the lessons of "Star Trek", if we were truly and deeply human.

It's very hard to fit into our society if you're different. Believe me. I know. It takes an immense amount of courage to figure out who you are, accept who you are, and truly be who you are. Most people never find that courage.

It also takes education, openness, and compassion to say, I don't understand this person or their choices, but I understand that this makes them happy. Who am I to deny another's happiness? Who am I to judge? Admittedly, I suck at the second part when it comes to conservative camouflage wearing people. Oh, I have compassion for them. It's miserable to carry around all that rage. It's sad that they deny themselves the true joy and pleasure of knowing some amazing people just because they don't agree with their lifestyle choices. So, I have compassion, but I cannot accept the choice to hate someone for being who they truly are.

Therefore, I cannot judge transgendered people. It takes more courage than I will ever have to make that decision. I cannot even begin to understand the agony of waking up every day thinking you're in the wrong body, not being able to be who you truly are, although I have woken up a few times wishing I had a penis, but that's another story.

So, my point is, before you open your mouth, open your mind; open your heart. Transgendered people are people, and all people need compassion, even those who wear camouflage.

God, I hate Father's Day almost as much as I hate Christmas. On his deathbed, I forgave my father for a lot of things. But Father's Day is still a sore spot because somewhere in my thirties I realized that I was never going to have any relationship with my father. I have friends who adore their fathers, who talk about them in glowing terms. It just seems alien to me. I cannot understand a loving, compassionate father although I clearly see them and know them. I get all Spock when I hear and see good fathers. I acknowledge it, but I can't feel it.

So, I'm going to give you some advice about being a dad from someone who recognizes the power you have to shape someone's life for good or evil. For the love of God, don't let your children turn out like me.

    1. Show up. If you're going to be in their life, be there. Don't come and go. But if you're going to be destructive, make the true act of sacrifice and just stay away. Better to be a ghost with possibilities than a demon with realities.

    2. Be loving. One of the great things about younger men is they grew up knowing it's okay to express and show love to their children.

    3. Treat women well. You are the man who will teach your children about men for good or evil. How you treat women will be how your daughter will think she deserves to be treated. How you treat women will teach your son how to treat women.

    4. If you do one through three, you'll be all right. Your kids love you, flaws and all.

Okay, I haven't said too much about the Penn State situation, but I think maybe you need to hear it from someone who has been there. At least once a semester, I have a student who comes to my office crying about something minor, only to have them reveal a history of sexual abuse. Naturally, I will refer them to counselors that will help, but I also listen to them, and I share my own history of sexual abuse.

For those of you who don't know, I was sexually abused by ten people, family members and family friends. So, before the Penn State situation was in the spotlight, I was comforting and helping students who are in agonizing pain, and now, after the Penn State situation, I've had to hear some rather insensitive comments and jokes. I've had to hear about poor Joe Paterno.

Every time I hear that, I think of their faces and their pain. I think of how often victims of sexual abuse are victimized again by this kind of brutal insensitivity. After years of therapy, I very seldom think about the abuse. It is what happened to me not who I am, but after days of hearing all about the abuse at Penn State, including some very graphic details, all of my emotions are raw and right on the surface.

So, if after reading this, you still think Joe Paterno and football are more important than a victim of sexual abuse, keep it to yourself and stay out of my life. I'm not a little girl anymore. I will not be victimized again, and I won't stand by and watch you victimize anyone else.

Finally, if you're a victim of sexual abuse, I urge you to get help. It's not your fault, and I promise you that it does get better; the pain does lessen, and you can go from feeling like a victim to being an empowered survivor.

I told my friend I was going to have one of those camps where you convert people, but instead of converting gay people, I'm converting conservatives into liberals.

First class, taking the Lord's name in vain.

Second class, vodka and other Jesus juice

Third class, Jesus didn't say that.

Fourth class, how a woman's body actually works.

Fifth class, Gaying it up

Now, before you say you'll have a camp to convert liberals, they already have that camp. It's called society, and I failed.

Chapter 19

Adventures in Teaching

I was teaching my students about Walt Whitman, how there's no proof he was gay.

I said, "He could have been. We just have no direct proof. He wasn't married and didn't have children, but that doesn't mean he was gay. I'm not married, and I have no children, and I'm not gay."

You should have seen their faces. I laughed out loud.

I said, "I see from your facial expressions that you thought I was."

Several of them nod.

"I'm not. Not that there's anything wrong with being gay."

Oh, I wished I had a camera.

Apparently, there's a bus that goes from the college to a local bar, The Woodside. My students were supposed to be doing group work, but I heard them talking about going to this bar.

I said, "Are you doing your work or talking about getting drunk at Woodside?"

Of course, they insisted they were doing their work.

I said, "Okay but for the record, I've been drunk at Woodside. That's how cool you are."

I'm packing up after my class, and three students from the next class walk in. One of them was a former student.

He says to his friend, "You had that teacher. He's the fat guy with the mustache."

The girl next to him says, "That's a lovely way to describe him."

I said, "Yeah, I don't want to know how you describe me."

He says, "I tell everyone you're the hot redhead."

That's hilarious.

I was wearing green and pink, and one of my students said, "Ms. Parker, you look nice. That's a good color combination."

I looked at him, and he said, "I'm being serious. You look like a Jolly Rancher, and I love Jolly Ranchers."

My student wrote a how-to paper. She used a specula, not a spatula, to crush the Oreos in her Oreo milkshake. No, I don't know why you'd use a spatula to crush Oreos either, but if it is a specula, I'm not drinking that milkshake.

One of the BEST lines I have ever read in a student paper. The topic was legalizing prostitution.

"Of course, I'm not talking about what you're all thinking. I'm not talking about the girl standing on the street corner waiting to be picked up and rode hard."

Today's quote, "Abraham Lincoln was working hard in the 1980s."

I bet he had a mullet, too.

This is how a student completed his poetry test today. Kudos to him for having the balls to basically say, I have no idea what you're talking about, and you sound like Charlie Brown's teacher to me. But this was not a correct answer.

"I'm sorry, I really don't know the parts/terms of poetry. As I was reading through the first part of the test, I could picture you standing in front of the class telling us about different terms. I just couldn't remember what you were saying as you were snapping your fingers and saying words like onomatopoeia. I'm sorry."

Seventeen students in my class today. Eight of them read and completed the assignment. I told the other nine to go home and come back when they were ready to participate in class, and then the remaining eight and I had a great discussion, one of the best I've had all semester.

I'm doing job interviews with my students in Tech Writing. I make them dress professionally.

This is the email I got. "I know that we are supposed to dress up for the interview, but I don't own any dress clothes. I intended to purchase some at Goodwill, but it doesn't look like I'm going to be able to afford to do so. I understand that you'll still need to deduct the points off of the assignment because I won't be fulfilling the requirements. You don't need to reply to this email. I just wanted to give you a heads up, so you're not caught off guard and disappointed when I come to the interview."

I responded and said to dress as nicely as he could.

But I bought the kid a gift certificate for Goodwill and told him to pick it up in my mailbox.

He never picked up the gift certificate.

He showed up for the interview and said, "I wanted to tell you this in person not in an email. I appreciate it, but I couldn't accept it because I didn't have money because I was irresponsible with my money. I partied too much and didn't have money. In fact, I'm not proud of how I did this semester at all. I'm moving off campus next year to eliminate some of my distractions."

I could have cried. How's that for maturity and taking responsibility for your actions? And he's only 20. There's hope for the future!

One of my female students reached over and grabbed the crotch of the guy next to her, right in front of me.

Me: Did you just do what I think you did?

Her: He dared me not to.

Me: So, you did it? No means no.

I was shocked, and not much shocks me.

Strangest thing I heard today

"I am into anime. Occasionally, I randomly speak Japanese. I just told you, so you wouldn't think I was nuts."

"Ms. Parker, I'm going to be late to class because I have to remove a tick."

I can't make this stuff up.

"I missed class because it was too cold and windy to walk up the hill."

I assume he means the very small hill on campus.

If I have to go to another teachers' meeting, I will poke my eye out with a fork.

I commented on their love of writing papers about Hitler this semester. I read like six in one weekend.

I said, "What is it with you people and Hitler?"

One of my students said, "He does have a cool mustache."

Chapter 20

Friends don't let friends mullet.

Can a man be attractive with a mustache, or is it always 70s-porn creepy?

Now, I'm googling Burt Reynolds' awesome 70s mustache.

That moment you're feeling pretty good about your beret until you realize you might look like Mama Fratelli from *The Goonies*.

I instantly mistrust anyone who wears their collar up. I've seen enough 80s movies to know someone is getting a wedgie.

Please do not follow the latest fashion trends. Not every man looks good with a beard, and most men do not look good with a hipster beard. You just look homeless and/or crazy.

My students and I were talking about 80s fashion, and I provided them with proof that some things should be left in the past.

Ladies and Gentlemen, may I present mullet time 1993? (Yeah, things move slower where I'm from.) Rock on!

Also, I'm pretty sure I'm covering my boobs because I'm wearing a see-through blouse, another great fashion choice.

Friends don't let friends mullet.

Chapter 21

Old Lady Things

I like young people. They still think things will work out. They think they can change the world.

Old people are trying to figure out how to never wear a bra again and how not to fart in public.

Forty-five is the magical age when all spicy food gives you heartburn, and you grow a beard.

I'm going to start a heavy metal band for middle-aged woman called Menopausal Rage.

Our first song-I will cut a bitch.

Oh my God, I've become my father. I'm sitting in my underwear, watching "M*A*S*H".

Someone just said, "I think you're my son's age."
I said, "How old is your son?"
He said, "30."
That was awesome!

I just got carded. That's right. They asked for my ID.

Okay, I was buying cough syrup at the pharmacy, but it's been years since I've been carded, so I'm feeling so young.

My sister, Tammy, said we should go out tonight and rip it up.

I said, "I'm old; I got a bad hip, and I'm fat like Honey Boo Boo's mama. I ain't ripping nothing."

If I get Alzheimer's...

A. Kill me

B. Don't drag me around to places apologizing for my behavior. My family does that now.

Some people are grateful for their nice house or fancy car.

I'm grateful for public restrooms.

That's right. I'm at the age where I think the best of humanity are the people who give an old woman a place to pee.

When I am old, I want to take bus trips with other old people. I want to make 80s references and laugh because only old people get it.

I want an old man who will carry my purse for me just because he loves me, and he doesn't care who knows it.

Of course, this is if my nudist colony and/or traveling in an RV retirement dream doesn't pan out.

Chapter 22

My therapist says...

My therapist says living in an RV is a perfectly acceptable lifestyle choice.

I love my therapist. I tell her about my man troubles.

She says, "It's like cocaine..." And begins a funny, but troubling, metaphor.

I was talking with my therapist about a man.

Me: I'm not sure why I put up with him.

Her: You wanted to get off.

Me: I wanted to be right.

Her: You wanted to get off and be right. All women want to get off and be right.

I agreed.

Then, later, she said my homework was to stop being easy.

Me: I really don't even want to try and date.

My therapist: If I had your dating history, I wouldn't either.

In the lobby of my therapist's office, she's saying good-bye to a little girl and her mother.

Little girl: I like to eat cardboard, paper, and erasers. They're good for my tummy.

My therapist and her mother try and convince her that they are not good for her tummy.

Me: (after I enter my therapist's office) I like to eat inappropriate things, too.

My therapist said I should invite a man over for dinner. Bad idea. Food poisoning is not sexy!

Conversations with my therapist

Me: I don't know if my problems stem from my bad decisions, or maybe I'm born under a bad sign.

Her: You internalize your problems too much. Maybe you should externalize a little. Go ahead. Blame it on the leprechauns or whatever.

Me: I don't think "blame it on the leprechauns" is good advice for a crazy person.

And we laughed.

Per my therapist, I'm not allowed to read and/or respond to Facebook comments for a while. Apparently, it's giving me a negative view of humanity.

Her: Do more productive things.

A blank stare from me

Her: Try to post and respond to positive things.

Me: Like kittens and babies?

Her: Yes or things that make you happy.

Pause

Her: Not penises

Me: Did you just tell me to buy a dildo?

Therapist: You don't get emotionally attached to electronics.

Pause

Therapist: This is going in the Facebook book; isn't it?

Me: Oh yeah.

Chapter 23

Encounters

I think I just inadvertently showed the pizza delivery boy my boob. That poor kid will have to get therapy.

At The Coal Miners' Cafe waiting for a friend
The waitress: Do you know what he'll drink?
Me: It's a she, but thanks for having confidence in me.

I was having lunch with a friend.

A guy walked in, and I stared at him.

Friend: Do you know him?

Me: I think I slept with him.

Friend: Don't you know?

Me: It's been awhile. I'd have to see his tattoos.

I do not have to leave my house for weird shit to happen to me.

On the 4th of July, my doorbell rang.

It was a state trooper. "Does Lawrence live here?"

Me: No.

Her: Is this apt 1?

Me: Yes.

Her: How long have you lived here?

Me: Since 2013.

Her: Do you know him?

She shows me his driver's license.

Me: No. Looks like Lawrence didn't change his address.

Her: Or he isn't around to.

She shows me that she's holding his driver's license and several credit cards.

Her: These were found with someone else.

Fuck, what the hell happened to Lawrence? Did someone kill him?

I went to Sheetz and ordered a meatball sub. The clerk who I know was holding the bag.

Me: You got my balls?

Her: Yeah, I massaged them real good for you.

Me: I like it when that happens.

Do other people have these conversations?

It was Christmas, and I was standing in line at the dollar store.

The lady in front of me turned around and said, "I can't wait until this fucking holiday is over."

I laughed.

And my sister thinks I act inappropriately in public.

Chapter 24

My friends and family will understand.

My niece said I cannot embarrass her in front of her college roommate. I believe she used the words, "loud" and "kooky".

Just realized I was standing in my living room wearing nothing but a pair of sandals. (Sorry for the visual.) How I came to be in this state of undress, I am not sure. I think it involved throwing what I was wearing into the washing machine, but one can never be sure.

I bought a shirt at the Goodwill. I wore it a few times before I noticed Joyce's name written on the inside of the shirt.

Clearly, Joyce was in the nursing room and is probably dead now.

But I look good in the shirt, and if I do something wrong, I can blame it on my haunted shirt.

I was dressed like a 1920s flapper for a murder mystery. Everyone complimented me about how good I looked.

When I explained why I was dressed that way, they all said, "Oh I thought you were just dressed like that, or I thought it was your artistic side."

Apparently, people expect wacky from me, and I do it so well.

I fell at work and injured my knee, and I had to use a scooter at Walmart.

After I got home, my brother walked into my apartment, looked at me, and said, "You're a 'Seinfeld' episode."

I always knew this day would come, the beginning of the end, so when I die, I'm enlisting one good, true, and honest person to stand up at my memorial service and say, "She was a fucking bitch," and then just sit down. Don't worry. My family and friends will understand.

Epilogue

Fifty-one-year-old woman available for immediate adoption. Highly educated and hilarious. Life would never be boring with this lovable tramp I mean scamp. Unfortunately, Barbara is broke as fuck and teetering on the edge of menopause. However, these problems are quite manageable with a job, chocolate, and a loving home.

Barbara needs to be the only fifty-one-year-old woman in the home as she tends to be rather loud and aggressive. Since Barbara is an older gal, the adoption fee will be waived.

Please help Barbara find her forever home, so she is no longer a vagabond reduced to laughing at her own jokes.

www.ingramcontent.com/pod-product-compliance
Lightning Source LLC
Chambersburg PA
CBHW071233080526
44587CB00013BA/1593